The Weading Feast

Storyline **Carol Fay Nicks**
Illustrations **Steven Butler**

Once Jesus told a parable about
ten maidens and a wedding. Five
of the maidens were wise, and
five were foolish. The ten maidens

put on their most beautiful clothes. They combed their hair carefully. Since it would be dark before the groom came, each one took a small lamp filled with oil.

Five of the maidens were wise. They took an extra jar of oil in case their lamps ran out. The other five maidens

were foolish. They didn't take any extra oil for their lamps. Now it was time to go to the wedding.

The maidens came to the place where they were to wait for the groom. But the groom was not there. He was very late. It was dark,

and the maidens became sleepy. They all sat down to wait. Soon all ten of the maidens fell fast asleep.

At midnight, there was a loud cry. "Here comes the groom!" someone shouted. "Wake up! Wake up! He is coming now!"

The maidens sat up and rubbed their eyes.
They looked at their lamps, but their lamps
were going out.

The five wise maidens poured their extra oil
into their lamps. Soon their lamps were burn-
ing brightly. But the five foolish maidens had

no extra oil. "Give us some of your oil," they
said to the five wise maidens. "Our lamps
are going out!"

"We can't," they replied. "We only have enough for our own lamps. Run quickly to the shops and buy some more." Then the

wise maidens joined the groom. The five
foolish maidens went to buy oil, but when
they came back, the door was locked!

"Let us in! Let us in!" they cried. But the groom said, "I do not know you." And he would not open the door. The five foolish

maidens were disappointed to miss the wedding. They were very sad they had not been ready to meet the groom.

"Remember this story," Jesus said to his friends. "I want you to be ready to meet me when I come."